Letters
to you,
to her,
to no one

Letters to you, to her, to no one

by
Vasilena Spasova

First published in paperback special edition, 2023
By Cybirdy Publishing Company
101 Camley Street, London NIC 4DU

This book is sold subject to the condition that it shall not, by way of trade, digitalisation or otherwise, be lent, resold, hired out or otherwise circulated without the publisher's prior consent in any form of binding or cover other than that in which it is published and without a similar condition being imposed on the subsequent purchaser.

Vasilena Spasova has asserted her right to be identified as the author of this work in accordance with the Copyright, Designs and Patents Act 1988

Translated by Vasilena Spasova
Cover design by Eva Vasileva
Edited by Afaf Shour

Illustrations by Atanas, Gergana, Nevrie, Rumen, Tsetsa & Violeta from Olga Skobeleva.

Printed by Hobbs the Printers Ltd

This book is typeset in Minion, Proxima Nova and Copperplate
A CIP record for this book is available from the British Library

ISBN: 978-1-7396637-2-8

Letters to you, to her, to no one

Vasilena Spasova

CYBIRDY
Publishing Limited

The orphanage

This is me. And who are you? Do you know me? Were you there for me when I took my first breath? Did you hold me tight when I opened my eyes for the first time? Did you take me into your arms, with your lips gently pressed on my forehead? Did you ever put your hand on my chest and feel my heartbeat? Did you feel the new life in me? This is me. And who are you? Were you ever a mother to me? You are unknown to me: a stranger, enigmatic and mysterious. The woman who gave me life.

How should I begin? What should I say? Countless thoughts, but no words. The pen glides on the white sheet. I am sitting here, tirelessly trying to tell the story behind one destiny. But my words are not enough. I wish I could open my soul to you—with no words, only feelings—to tell you about my life. This is me. And who are you?

Would you be able to recognise me if you saw me after all these years? People say that no one forgets their child's eyes. Do you remember mine? My life has turned from hope to dust. And now, all alone, I am desperately trying to build a new life for myself. This is me, and who are you?

Will I ever see you again? Will I ever have the chance to tell you about my life trapped within these four walls where the mother figure is nothing but a mirage? Where dozens of children's hearts are brought together, patiently waiting for her, the only one in the world: the mother.

This is me, and who are you?

The unsent letters

I love the paper, especially the newsprint. I like how the ink smoothly flows onto the sheet and leaves a trail that can never be erased. Even if you try to delete each letter with a rubber, each word, it will always leave its mark. The sunbeams will shine on the seemingly clean sheet, and all traces of once-written words will reappear. All the words will reappear, and they will tell the story of a person who found the strength to bare their soul and take the biggest risk someone can by allowing themself to be vulnerable. I've always been afraid of that. I've always been afraid of letters. Because most often, we write letters when we are hurt, when we suffer, when we love unconditionally or when we are indescribably happy. I don't mean those businesslike letters, which we sit down to write with such hostility and reluctance simply because we have to, because 'real life' requires us to do so. I mean these letters we write to our parents, to friends or to a beloved person. I'm afraid of these letters.

You sit in a small dark room in the evening, with just the rusty old-fashioned bedside lamp lighting the space. The light illuminates your face, revealing every wrinkle, every scar on it. Neither anxiety, happiness, love, nor hate can be hidden from the yellowish-white bulb. Quite self-conscious, without anyone's pressure, you sit alone with your soul, with your heart, with all your secret thoughts and feelings, which you are sometimes afraid of, and begin writing. Word by word, line after line, you pour out everything you have in you and everything you have kept to yourself for a long time. You've been writing and writing until the point you are left with no breath. As if your mind has abandoned you from exhaustion, and even you yourself don't know where you are and whether you exist at all. You put down the pen and take the sheet in your hand. You fold it one time, and then you fold it again,

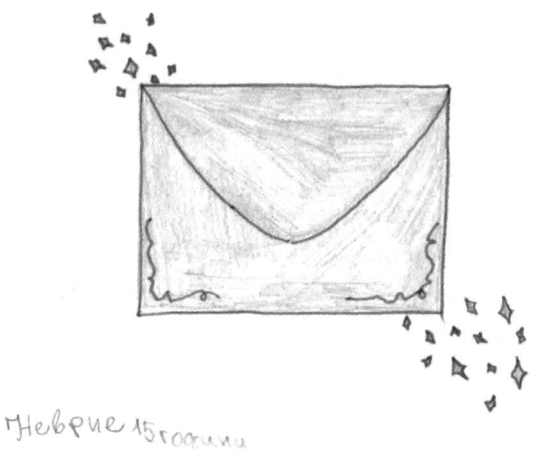

tenderly putting it into an empty white envelope. You touch the envelope with your lips, leaving part of yourself on it, seal the envelope and, stretching your hand, you take the blue pen and carefully write the name of the one who will judge you. You reveal your nature and put the darkest parts of your soul on display, praying that your vulnerability isn't used against you and that you aren't destroyed for it. If not by that person, then surely waiting for the words, which will never come, is what will slowly crush you. These letters, the sent ones, are what I'm most afraid of.

I met Nikolay quite by accident. It was a week after I had left the orphanage, and I was at the station, waiting for the train that would take me to the little village in South Bulgaria I was living in at the time. It was in the afternoon in late September. The wind was gently blowing and spreading the scent of the approaching autumn. He was a man in his late forties, neatly dressed, with a dark green sweater and a brown leather bag with a few sheets of paper sticking out from it. I was watching him with interest. He was not like the others; there was something different about him. He was not looking around, lifting his eyes to watch the strangers passing by. He had his head bent as he propped a sheet of paper on his knee and wrote. Five, ten, fifteen minutes passed, and he didn't stop writing. His hand seemed to have merged with the sheet and the pen, and he couldn't get away even for a moment.

I was sitting on the bench beside him, trying not to stare, but apparently, I had drifted off for a moment. He suddenly put down the blue pen and looked straight at me.

I was so startled that I didn't even manage to avert my eyes and pretend that I hadn't been watching him all this time.

"Sorry. I didn't want to gaze in that direction and watch you. Sorry. Excuse me."

I felt so awkward that the only words I could say at that time were "sorry" and "regret". I repeated them so many times that, at one point, he burst into uncontrollable laughter.

"It's OK. Don't worry about it. Perhaps I'd be watching in the exact same way if I were you."

He didn't speak to me using the plural form of "you" in Bulgarian, which was considered polite, and I liked it. I had met him just a few minutes ago, but after the second sentence, I already felt close to him. And I began laughing with him. Just like that, for no reason.

"Sorry for being curious, but I can't help but ask: what are you writing?"

He didn't pause, even for a moment. "Letters". He was looking straight into my eyes and smiling.

"Letters? And to whom?" My curiosity had already reached such proportions that I couldn't stop asking questions.

"To somebody and to no one" were his exact words.

I didn't have the slightest idea what he had in mind and

what to say. I was just sitting and looking at him with bewilderment. His next words stayed in my mind for a long time, and they've helped me overcome my fear and are the reason I'm now able to write all these letters to you, Mum. His words sound so clear in my mind, as if he has just uttered them.

"These letters are addressed to my ex-wife. Five years ago, she left me and went abroad with our son. And I haven't seen him since. Once a week, we talk over the phone, but I haven't seen either him or her for almost five years now. How much has he grown up? How much has she changed? Has she got older, or is she still the same as I remember? Our separation was hard on both of us. With a lot of words said and many unspoken, with much pain and wasted opportunities. That's why I started to write her letters. I tell her about my day, my feelings, the present and the past. About all those things that I couldn't tell her while she was standing face-to-face in front of me. About everything I felt that my male pride never allowed me to express. It's why I now describe all these things on these sheets of paper."

He paused for a moment and took the letter into his hands. His eyes began to wander indiscriminately on the sheet; he folded it and put it in the worn leather bag.

"But I'll never send them. That's why I said that they are to someone and to no one. When questions become too much, and the pain outweighs to such an extent that it seems to suck all the energy out of your life, then you sit down and write. You open up your soul and say the most terrifying words without any fear. And when you're satisfied, and the burden falls off your chest, then you fold the paper and put it in the drawer with the rest of the letters. Without fear of the answer. Without the much-anticipated but never arriving replies. Without the answer, full of misunderstandings and meaningless accusations. Only with the easiness in the chest. Finally, you've said all that you've kept for so long hidden inside, even though there is no one to hear you."

The steam locomotive whistled. Suddenly, he grabbed his bag and ran to the track. "See you soon. Have a nice day!"

At that moment, I fell in love with letters, especially unsent ones. I found a way to talk to you, Mum, without fear, without expectations, but to tell you all that I've always needed to share with you.

I want you to go through the worst

He had the darkest brown—almost black—eyes I had ever seen. His eyebrows were even darker. The deep furrow that ran across his forehead and his aquiline nose gave his appearance a respectable seriousness and austerity. For three weeks, since he started working as a guard at the orphanage, we hadn't spoken a word. Every time I left for school or came back, I passed by him so fast that even if he wanted to say something, I didn't give him the chance.

Mum, I didn't mean to be rude to the newcomer, but I thought he was an angry old man who was just waiting to talk to you and give a long speech about how young people today are good for nothing and the country has nothing else to be 'proud of' except for its corrupt rulers. I had heard those words hundreds of times on the bus going to school, and I didn't want to hear them again.

But as I later learned, I shouldn't have jumped to such conclusions.

Fate brought me face-to-face with him one late afternoon. At that moment, I really needed a friendly word.

That's when I really needed you, Mum.

But he was there in your place. He made it his responsibility to teach me an important life lesson. That's exactly what a true parent would do.

We were over forty children living in the orphanage. Each one of us with our own pains, hopes, insecurities and dreams. All kinds of emotions coexisted within us, and nobody ever knew which of these emotions would prevail at any given moment. That afternoon, I thought the pain got the better of me. It was not only my own but the obsessive pain and loss felt by the children at the orphanage who had played a cruel trick on me.

I will soon tell you about this incident in which, without realising it, you also took part. But now, let's return to my acquaintance with Atanas.

After three weeks and not a word exchanged, I learned his name. And it became one of my favourite names. And this seemingly stern stranger turned out to be one of my truest friends.

I sat under a huge oak tree just behind the military unit. My face was burning, my whole body was shaking, and tears were streaming down my cheeks. Atanas had seen everything that happened that fateful afternoon. He approached me slowly, with a light, comforting smile, and sat next to me under the tree. For more than five minutes, we sat like that without saying anything to one another. I was crying, and he was just sitting next to me.

And then he told me, "I was twenty-two when I became a father to a baby girl. She was born at the perfect weight and size and, uncharacteristically for a baby, with thick, dark hair. When she was little, people said she looked just like me. When she grew up and went to school, everyone suddenly declared that she was her mother's spitting image. I think so, too. She has her colourful eyes and milky white skin.

At twenty-two, you're pretty young to be a parent, don't you think? You have to be ready, not only to take responsibility but ready with enough knowledge about life to give the best to your child. I was lucky enough to not fear this responsibility. On the contrary, I was extremely happy and proud of the fact that I had become a father. And as with anyone still at the beginning of life's journey, I had no idea what I was doing. But I didn't realise it at the time.

I found that out fifteen years later, on the night I got a call from the hospital emergency room. I got goosebumps. It felt as if the world had broken into a million pieces, and I was completely powerless to do anything. My little daughter, whom I had watched over like an eagle for fifteen years, was hit by a car on her way home from school. How could I have let this happen? Why wasn't I there to protect her? To protect her, as I had always done until then.

All the way to the hospital, I kept spewing insults and accusations at myself. If you knew how much I hated myself that day… When I saw her lying in the hospital bed with her leg in a cast and several stitches on her forehead, I couldn't hold back my tears and cried like a little child. I cried aloud. And she, my defenceless little princess, smiled and stretched out her arms to me.

She gave me a big hug and said, 'It's going to be OK, Dad. Don't cry. Everything will be fine.' She was the one who needed comfort and care at that moment, but instead, she was thinking of me. That day, I realised something that I seemed to have missed. I didn't understand how or when my little girl had become a conscious person. The next day, we were handed two heavy wooden crutches and an ampoule of liquid Analgin and were discharged from the hospital. She didn't say a word. She didn't complain even once for two whole months. On the second day, she was able to move around the house by herself without asking anyone for help. As if she had become a different person after that incident. Overnight, she had become stronger than before. And she had no intention of surrendering.

For fifteen years, I prayed every night that nothing bad would happen to my child. I prayed that she would go through this life untouched by its cruel hand. But I finally realised that this was the worst thing I could have asked for my child. So, from that moment on, I began to pray that my daughter would go through as many difficulties and obstacles as possible and that after each successive failure, she would stand up stronger, yearning for life."

Atanas finished his story, and that was how he became a true friend and teacher to me. I hugged him tightly as a daughter would hug her father.

This short letter is not addressed to you, Mum, but perhaps you could recognise yourself in it.

The letter which I never received

My dear child,

I want you to smile. Just like that, for no reason.

I want you to be unable to tell the story to your friends because every time you try to speak, you'll start laughing, unable to catch your breath, and your friends will stare at you in bewilderment.

I want you to give me a big hug. With both arms, as any real hug should be.

I want your eyes to shine when you listen to music and look out the car window, dreaming of a million things.

My dear child, even more sincerely, I want you to cry, to wander hopelessly, looking for the littlest hope left in your life. I want you to spend days alone, with nobody around. No shoulder to cry on and no friend to talk to. I want you to lose everything, even yourself.

I want you to fall on your knees, bruise yourself on the sharp edges of life, and not get up for days.

I want you to feel happiness, but just as badly, I want you to feel pain. Only when you go through these things do you become a grown, strong and brave person whom I'll be proud of and love without limits until the end of my days.

I love you! Even though I don't know you!

The trick

Hi Mum,

Do you like magic tricks? Do you immerse yourself in magic, or are you the type of person who's always looking for a rational explanation? I didn't believe in magic tricks until Georgi, a ten-year-old boy with dark hair and brownish-green eyes, came to the orphanage. We became friends as soon as he arrived. From then on, he was part of "our big family," as one of the educators once said. I know he meant it in a good way, and he probably had a point too.

There was something Georgi and I called 'the trick'. He would look at me, wink, and say with a smile: "Come on, now. Let's do the trick."

He didn't even have to say those words. Just a look, a small smile, and I knew it was time to act. You must be wondering what I'm talking about, Mum. What is this trick?

The trick, Mum, is a small gesture, maybe even an insignificant one. A naive child's joke, or, as we liked to call it, magic. Over the years, Mum, the more things I see in my life, the more I realise that the trick was one of the truest things.

Ina was our age. An eleven-year-old girl with light brown hair and dark brown eyes. She didn't communicate much with Georgi and me; we were in different friend groups, if such a thing could even exist in an orphanage.

But Georgi liked her very much. And you know, Mum, he wasn't afraid to show it. He was only a child, but he was so brave. He wasn't afraid to bare his soul, to share his feelings with the world.

What if he receives nothing back? What if his feelings remain unrequited, and he only exposes himself by allowing himself to be vulnerable?

That's what I loved most about him. He wanted nothing in return. When he did something good, no matter how small or how big it was, he never looked back. He didn't wait for thanks; he wanted neither recognition nor encouragement. He didn't expect the same in return. He just wanted to give himself away, and that was quite enough for him.

Ina paid him no attention. She didn't return his smiles; sometimes, she didn't even greet him back. But he didn't get sad. And so, every day until the very end, he always greeted her kindly, never missing an opportunity to innocently smile and meet her gaze. Even though they didn't talk often, hardly ever really, he always knew when she was sad.

That was when he would look at me and say: "It's time for the trick."

The trick was most often performed outside when there were many children around. It was the most suitable setting so that the illusion wouldn't be revealed. Ina often sat on the old rusty swing in the orphanage yard. The screeching of rusted bolts could drive you crazy, but, as Georgi said, it was his favourite sound.

He would approach her without saying a word. She would look up and ask him what he wanted. Her eyes would be red, with trails of dried tears on her skin.

"Do you believe in magic?"

She wouldn't answer, only continue to stare at him.

"No? Now you will. Do you like flowers? Do you like roses more specifically?"

She'd look at him in confusion. At least the first few times.

"Now, look."

George would begin to wave his right hand and mutter some magical, completely invented words, without which the magic could not be done.

Now the most important moment would come. While he taunted Ina with some newly composed spell, I would run out, pluck a rose from the yard next door, and quite casually, without giving myself away in any way, blend in with the children roaming about the yard and slowly walk up behind Georgi. That was the climax, and we couldn't fail. If we were discovered, our whole trick would lose its meaning. His right hand would still be waving, while his left hand stayed ready behind his back. I would walk behind him and, in a split second, hand him the torn rose.

And *voila*!

He'd pull out the rose as if from nowhere and hand it to Ina. Was it because we were kids, or did the trick really work? Either way, she always gasped. And as sad as she had been that day, as soon as we did the magic trick, she would be smiling.

That's what I'm talking about, Mum. That is the great trick. It is actually something very simple, and despite the preparation involved, the trick was indeed magic.

Because something that brings a smile to someone's heart is the greatest magic in this world, Mum.

Bugaeja — 14

Vanilla ice cream with chocolate chips
(the death of Mitko)

Hi Mum.

My legs can't hold me any longer, my heart is beating hundreds of beats per minute, and my head is getting heavier and heavier, but I keep running with all my might until I finally stumble and fall to the ground. I don't have the strength to stand up anymore. I don't want to stand up anymore.

It's two in the morning. I've just woken up from another nightmare, but it was no different than the one yesterday or the one the night before. And maybe after all these years, I've become used to them. As if they aren't so scary any more. As a mother would say: "It's just a nightmare. It isn't real."

Unfortunately, this was real. A true story that happened nine years ago.

Do you like ice cream, Mum? I adore it. Mitko also loved it, though he always chose vanilla over chocolate, which I never understood. He was a strange boy, but he was my friend, even though he obviously knew nothing about ice cream.

The end of the month was special, and every child at the

orphanage waited for it with great anticipation. On every twenty-fifth of the month, each of us received a payment, which we called a 'salary'. It was how we joked with each other. The money wasn't much, but we didn't want more. Living in an orphanage had taught us that even a little was more than enough. Mitko and I ran up to the teacher on duty and began persistently asking for permission to go to the ice cream shop. She refused us many times because we, the 'little ones', weren't allowed to step outside the orphanage without being accompanied by an adult.

Виолета—14

After about twenty minutes of constant grumbling, tears, pleas and many promises, which of course, we knew wouldn't be kept, the manager was finally willing to let us go. I remember the joy I felt the moment she spoke the words: "OK. Go!"

Words that I later wished I hadn't heard.

We ran out of the orphanage. Our hearts were pounding, either because of the running or because of the anticipation over what ice cream flavour we were going to choose.

Choose… choice. We had a choice.

Mum, can you imagine what having a choice meant to us? Never mind that I'm just referring to ice cream. We, the children with no choice, could choose at that moment.

The shop was not far from the orphanage at all, but the sun was so hot, and our feet were fidgety with impatience. So, Mitko and I decided to shorten our route and go through one of the back streets. As we walked, we listed all possible types of ice cream and had already decided which ones we were going to get.

Yes, we knew the entire shop assortment by heart. We often passed by, staring at the windows and fantasising about the ice cream we would have bought if we had the money. But in most cases, we didn't have anything, so we only made a note of what to buy next time.

The alley was lonely. The sun had reached its highest point, and people had taken shelter in their homes. I still remember the scream. The horror in Mitko's voice still seems to echo over and over and over again in my mind. Two older boys, apparently in their twenties, were standing in front of us, blocking our way. One of them grabbed Mitko by the collar of his dark green blouse (his favourite shirt, which he had put on for our special ice cream day) and began to violently push him again and again against the wall.

"Give me the money! Give me the money!" the bully shouted. Mitko had a twenty leva note clutched in his hand and would not let it go.

"Give it!" the slightly taller boy said. I could see rage and uncontrollable anger in his eyes.

"Leave him alone! Here! Take that!" I cried and threw my ten leva note onto the ground.

Mitko was stronger than me. He was a year older and didn't like to obey anyone, even the strictest educators at the orphanage, which often got him into trouble. He swung once, to no avail. He then swung a second time, harnessing all his strength in his otherwise skinny arm, and hit the boy who was pinning him to the stone wall.

Blood suddenly ran down his nose, dripping along his chin, and large drops fell to the ground. At that moment, I realised what people meant when they compared somebody to a raging bull. Just like the animal, blow after blow mercilessly knocked Mitko to the ground again and again. His frail body convulsed with every blow. The kicks cut into his chest, his head, and his back like knives. His screams of relentless pain were deafening.

My heart couldn't stand it. It was as if the fear had disappeared, and I had nothing more to lose at that moment. I sprang upon our tormentors.

"Stop! Leave him alone!"

But my moment of bravery lasted only a few seconds, and before I realised it, I was lying on the ground next to Mitko. I curled up into a ball and held out my hand to my dear friend.

I gripped his arm tightly like a drowning man clutching his life raft. But at that moment, I could no longer hear the cries. There was no trace of the piercing screams that had been continuous until now. It was silent, and Mitko's dark green eyes were closed.

That was the last day I heard his voice. Hand in hand, two on the grey concrete, him and I.

And we, Mum…

We had just wanted some vanilla ice cream with chocolate chips. We hadn't wanted anything more out of life, but life surprised us.

The red sock

Hi Mum,

Isn't it remarkable how we can sometimes find inspiration in the smallest of things? No, I'm not talking about the kind gestures, the smiles exchanged with a stranger on the road, the advantage someone gave us, or the hug of a dear friend. I'm talking about the really small, insignificant things, like a nondescript sock. I know, I really know it sounds crazy, and it probably is. But today, at twenty-three years old, I was inspired by a slightly worn-out red sock.

The night was long. The wind was raging, and the rain hadn't stopped for two days now. My eyes burned from exhaustion, but I couldn't sleep. It was as if the more I tried to banish my thoughts, the more they multiplied and gave me no rest. After over an hour of trying to sleep, I decided to get up and do something useful.

Of course, I had to be careful not to make too much noise and not to wake up Theodora. What better activity was there to do at midnight than running the washing machine. I know what you're thinking. It isn't the quietest activity, but our flat was equipped with the latest washing machine, which made very little noise. I think it has to be the most valuable thing Theodora and I own. If we were ever robbed, the first thing I'd check on would be the washing machine.

While at the orphanage, Mitko and I loved to play soldiers on a secret mission, which involved a lot of crawling on the floor, climbing, sometimes falling, and lots of bruises, torn blouses, and hard-to-wash stains. We were very good at this game! Well, of course, the teachers punished us afterwards because, according to them, it was a show of absolute disrespect to their work and the things that were provided to us, but the truth is that it was our escape from reality. Crawling on the floor with a branch in hand and a half-cut football on our heads instead of a helmet, we were children in the full sense of the word. Just like any other child who'd come home covered in dirt and be punished by their parents.

Vanity is not a feeling I often experience, but I have loved the smell of clean clothes ever since I was a child. It was comforting. Sometimes I would close my eyes and imagine you were tightly hugging me, and I could smell your favourite perfume mixed with the lilac washing powder you always liked to use. Not that other washing powders were bad, but you felt that this particular scent suited you best, and it wasn't overpowering. I don't know if any of that is true, but since I was a child, I liked to imagine what kind of things you liked, the way you might frown when you got angry at

some wild thing I'd done. But you absolutely refuse to use any anti-wrinkle cream because you believe that they give a person character and are something to be proud of, not try to hide.

Can you see? I'm doing it again. I'm thinking of you, Mum. I think about you every day.

After Theodora and I settled in this flat, I saved money for several months to buy a nice washing machine so I could always feel this cosiness. I have to admit that Theodora is better at using it than I am, but I've learned quite a bit, too. Well, sort of. You wouldn't believe the look on her face when

I first decided to do laundry and stuffed all the clothes into the washing machine without even thinking about separating them by colour.

I ran the washing machine, warmed up a glass of milk and sat on the small couch in the living room. I don't remember when I managed to drift off, but I didn't wake up until the morning. Theodora wasn't up yet, and I decided to use that time alone to lay out the clothes and then make a breakfast that she wouldn't even touch. But I had to try anyway. I opened the washing machine door, and to my great surprise, all the white clothes had become pale pink. Even Theodora's favourite dress, which she adored but only wore at home because she thought people would judge, and I quote, her "massive calves like those of a sixty-year-old ex-bodybuilder."

At first, I was angry at my own carelessness. Theodora always reminds me to check that there isn't anything left in the drum before I start the next wash.

Well, Teddy, yes, there was an old red sock left, which added colour to all our white clothes. The dress was still pretty. It would even suit her skin better. After I stopped being angry and fidgeting around with the washing machine as if that would make a difference, I came up with an idea.

Mum, you know I like writing. I don't know if I'm any good at it or not, but I do it with great love, and it brings me real satisfaction. And at that somewhat ridiculous moment, I got an idea for a poem dedicated to Theodora. She liked it very much. I hope you'd like it too, Mum.

Hello,
That's how all stories begin.
Or none.
There is only one star visible in the sky tonight.
But it doesn't look empty. Not at all.
It's as if it's lit even brighter than before.
The star shines just above the porch of the log house
And pines gently sway by the light wind.
The third step of the stairs outside the front door
is still creaking.
And the scratch on the door since that summer evening,
spent dancing and having a few drinks,
when the lock seemed to constantly keep changing its place.
The little hole left in the rug in front of the fireplace
from your first attempt
at starting a fire that cold winter night.
The turquoise blue room that you painted yourself
and you really like it
even though it doesn't match the rest of the walls at all.
But it blends so well with the colour of your crystal blue eyes.
The small crack in the tiles on the kitchen floor

when you dropped the hot pot
of freshly cooked pasta and homemade sauce.
The most delicious pasta anyone had ever made.
The withered orchid you refuse to throw away
because you believe that one day it will bloom again.
The old radio that blares, but you prefer above all others
because the rustling somehow gives a deeper emotion
to the sound.
And of course, your favourite light pink dress,
which used to be white, but I didn't see the red sock at the
bottom of the washing machine.
How beautiful it looks on you.
You are all these things.

I still remember that day, the 21st of December. It was the coldest day of the year, and I later learned that it had been the coldest one in Bulgaria in the last five years. The streets were empty, most of the shops had already closed, and very few cars drove through the snowy streets.

The orphanage wasn't too far away, but the wind blew so hard that every step I took felt like I was taking ten. I walked towards the bus stop, and to my surprise, there was another person out on the streets on this cold day. It was Theodora. She wore an oversized, bright orange jacket, a green beanie, and the longest scarf I'd ever seen in my life. Later, she told me that it had been a present from her grandmother, who had passed away five months ago. It was supposed to be Theodora's Christmas gift, but her grandmother had given it to her in August. Theodora laughed with teary eyes while telling me that story.

"Who gives you a winter scarf in August?" She wiped away the tear falling down her cheek. "Perhaps the same person who always knew what to say when you had a bad day. Even on the worst days, she found something positive to say. Once, I had a terrible allergic reaction, and my eyes were so swollen I could barely keep them open. But she looked at me and said that my hair looked wonderful today. Her words could heal you on the hardest days."

Theodora often spoke of her grandmother. She hoped that one day she would be at least half as good a person as her grandma. I think she achieved that and much more.

I sat on the bench next to Theodora. She smiled and greeted me. That was when I saw that she had a small brown puppy curled up in her lap. Theodora loved all animals, especially dogs. She told me that she had found the little stray on the street, shaking and almost completely covered in snow. So she decided to take it and offer it temporary shelter in her arms. She was visibly freezing, but he needed a warm place to rest, and she was there for him. She didn't know how long she was going to stay at the bus stop or where she was going to take the puppy afterwards, but it didn't matter to her. She said that, right now, they both felt calm and happy, and that was all that mattered.

That was the very first thing that I noticed about Theodora, and she continued to impress me throughout the years of our friendship. She never took anything for granted. She enjoyed the simple things: a hug after a long day, a warm cup of tea during a stormy day, a favourite book that she had read dozens of times before, or a little stray puppy curled up in her arms.

The bus arrived an hour later than it was meant to, but we didn't mind. The time had flown by while we were talking about all sorts of things: books, dogs, photography, the stars, and the universe. It felt like we'd been friends forever, though we'd just met an hour ago. From that moment on, we spent every day together, and we never ran out of things to talk about. Since then, I never minded if the bus was late. Sometimes, a delay could lead to the start of a beautiful friendship.

Note: Perhaps, at times, this story is chaotic, disjointed, and even quite confusing. If so, then I've managed to describe it as truthfully as it really is. Because this is life, and it isn't in order at all. Not at all.

As you already know, after my brief meeting with Nikolay, I really fell in love with letters, especially unsent ones. In them, I found comfort and freedom to be myself without fear.

That's why I decided to collect a few letters from various people, both known and unknown to me. I've asked them to write these letters in order to share them with you here, among the pages of my life.

Perhaps some of them will make you laugh, and others may even make you cry; I don't know, but I do know they will make you feel, and that is the most wonderful thing about letters.

I collected them to distract you, Mum, so that you don't feel the bitterness of my life, at least for a little while!

That could be in a letter to you, but at another time, under other circumstances!

Miss you…

From Annie (to her mother)

Hi, Mum!

A girl older than me asked if I wanted to write you a letter. I haven't written a letter before, but she is helping me. It's actually pretty fun, but you might be angry when you read it.

Do you remember on Tuesday when you had to stay late at work and told me to get home on time and prepare for the Maths test? And when you came back, I told you I had done all my homework? It wasn't quite true. Actually, the whole story was a lie.

I got home five minutes before you, put on my house clothes and pulled out the first textbook I saw. I know you had taught me that I shouldn't lie under any circumstances, especially not to you.

That's why I'm writing this letter to you to apologise.

You have told me that it's never too late to correct a mistake. So, I hope you won't get mad. And also, you won't be mad at Dad for watching a football game and eating chips on the couch all night. I didn't want to betray him, but he wasn't very obedient either, and he was much older than me. But he was

ATHHNC - 11

happy with the game, and at the end, he was excitedly waving a long scarf around the living room.

I don't know how long a letter should be, I think it is enough. However, before I tell you how much I love you and that, finally, I've put my room in order, I have to admit one last thing.

That same day I went out without a jacket, even though you had warned me not to. The good thing is that it turned out that you had been completely right. I should have dressed warmer. So, the bad thing is that now my throat hurts. But I played basketball with the older kids, and I scored a point! Can you believe it, Mum? They said they would call me to play with them again. But this time, if the weather is bad, I'll put on my jacket, I promise.

Thank you for everything you do for me, Dad and our cat Ronnie, who, unfortunately, ate your orchid. And I got a poor grade in Maths.

Lots and lots, and lots, and lots of love,

Annie

What did I do?

Hi Mum!

If only you could have seen how happy Theodora was today! I hadn't seen her smile for a long time, and I missed it so much. However, during the last few months, even when she smiled, it cost her too much strength. Strength that she no longer had to spare.

But today… Today she was really happy, Mum. What about me? I did something terrible. Mum, would you forgive me if you knew why I had done it? Do all the excuses I could list matter if what I did hurt another person?

Please forgive me, Mum. At least you do, because I won't be able to.

The woman was walking with difficulty, leaning on a wooden cane and a wheeled shopping trolley which she was just barely pushing. Her hair was grey and cut short like most women her age. I did not see her face. Not because I couldn't but simply because I didn't want to. It's easier to do something bad to someone whose face you've never seen. You don't remember their features, so they can't appear and haunt you in your nightmares. It's as if what you did never happened.

But it happened. And I know it.

I passed by the pension office, where every fortnight, dozens of elderly people lined up waiting for their measly pensions. Then they stopped at the corner shop but only bought essentials. It was one of the few remaining small shops that still gave out goods on the so-called 'informal loan', trusting the customers. A large notebook with a thick cover was lying on the cash desk, and all debts were recorded in it.

For the past year, I had passed by this shop on my way to the hospital almost every day, and I already knew the features of the neighbourhood. But all that time, I never suspected, even for a moment, what was about to happen.

After she must have been waiting in line for hours, the elderly woman managed to get out of the crowd and slowly, pushing the cart and leaning on the cane, made her way to the nearest bus stop. Let's call her the 'Unsuspecting woman'. That is the name I gave her in my mind.

That was because, on that day, she never suspected that someone would steal her pension. Neither of us would have guessed that the someone in question would be me.

Walking, she swayed slightly from side to side, trying to stay as steady as possible. I saw her purse slipping out of the pocket of her worn fur coat already.

Yes, Mum. It happened exactly as you might think. I took

the purse and didn't try to catch up to its owner. I didn't touch her lightly on the shoulder so as not to startle her. I didn't apologise for the trouble and didn't hand her the dark red purse with a coin pocket.

She didn't hug me and tell me I was a very nice child.

Because I am not. Or at least, I wasn't on that day.

Mum, do bad deeds define bad people? Is it possible for a good person to do such a terrible thing?

I remember the next moment; I ran and hid behind a building like some seasoned thief. I took out the money and threw the purse onto the ground, and it fell right into a muddy puddle with all my dignity and convictions.

Now you must be asking, what was the money for? To buy medicine for Theodora? I didn't spend it on medicine, Mum. It could never make her so genuinely happy.

Theodora was in love with photography. She didn't believe she had any talent but still dreamed of being a professional photographer one day. But not for recognition, exhibitions, or awards. She always said she wanted to take pictures of living life.

She said she wanted to capture as many real smiles as possible.

She would measure her own success by the number of smiles.

I like that about her, Mum. I like her dreams. They are quite simple and clear. Perhaps all dreams should be like that.

Черника - 8г.

I went into the pawn shop, which was two blocks away from the hospital. A few weeks ago, they had a very nice camera on display. I didn't know a lot about equipment, but I knew for sure that this brand was Theodora's favourite.

Exactly two hundred and thirty-five leva.

I took the crumpled notes out of my pocket and handed them to the cashier. The burden stuck to my chest grew heavier.

If only you could have seen how happy Theodora was. Getting up was too difficult for her, but I managed to convince the nurse to give us a wheelchair to go out into the yard. I pushed her, running from one end of the yard to the other.

And Theodora was laughing, laughing like a little child. And she would only stop me when she wanted to take a picture of something.

She took a picture of me, too. She said she finally managed to catch my smile.

Please forgive me, Mum. At least you. Because I won't forgive myself.

From him to her with lots of love and a sense of humour
(let's take the pressure off a bit)

You'll find this note pinned to the fridge next to all the drawings of our son (I think that most of them are doodles) and the family portrait (I won't even comment on it today. I'll just say that the family portrait is a family portrait precisely because the cheeky neighbours have no place in it. Anyway, at least the turkey they brought over was worth it).

And I know, I really know, that I have to encourage the child. And I'm really trying, but let's be realistic. This looks more like a taco than a sports car, a hybrid at that.

Also, on that line of thought, I have to tell you honestly that the colour of the dress you are wearing in the 'family, not-quite-family portrait' as I call it does not suit anyone. Even you. Even though everything suits you.

I don't even want to get to that part because now you're going to get very angry, but I have to admit something to you. I broke your favourite vase that your grandmother had given you and that you were planning to give to our grandchildren, and hopefully, them to their grandchildren, and so on, until someone made a rational decision and put it up for sale on the internet.

Well, this vase was passed down through generations. A tradition you told me about several times, but I never understood. In fact, there are many things I don't understand about your family.

For example, why does your father always ask for my opinion on the economic development of the country and then refute every statement I make?

Or why does your mother separate clothes so precisely when colour-catching wipes exist? A genius invention, by the way.

Or why must the annoying neighbours and their even more annoying cat be in our family portrait? Isn't it meant to be a *family* portrait?!

You're right; I got a little off-topic. I'll get to the point.

As I've said, someone (I say "someone", but as I mentioned earlier, I mean "I") broke the vase in question. That was when our son looked at me with such pity that I didn't even know a seven-year-old child could feel and told me:

"Don't worry. We'll tell Mum that I broke it. She'll get angrier at you."

"What? How could she get angrier at me?"

"You're a grown-up man, and you should have learned by

now to be more careful and not break things," Picasso Jr. continued to explain to me. "Especially Mum's things."

I admit that playing fetch with the dog inside the house wasn't the best idea.

Our son wanted to sacrifice himself and take the blame for me! Meanwhile, there I was, trying to stage a robbery. Believable, I know. Probably as believable as the time you swore that, no, you hadn't bought those extra blouses and shoes; the saleswoman must have slipped them into your bag by accident.

Now I'm going out, and I will be back later. I'm going to lie down on the couch, but if you happen to change your mind and aren't too angry at me, I'd be happy if you let me sleep next to you. Because to wake up next to you is the best feeling in the world. It's everything to me.

PS: I was going to stage a robbery.

To let you go

Hi Mum,

I'm writing to you from the clinic's waiting room. Theodora is here beside me, leaning her head on my shoulder. I'm holding her cold hand, bruised from all the cannulas, and with my other hand, I'm writing the next letter to you. Her breathing is so quiet, almost imperceptible. The doctors say that her heart rate is much slower than normal, and every day, it slows down more and more because her body is exhausted. Every day, little by little, she is leaving me.

And I'm so desperately clinging to her.

I can't let her go, Mum. I'm just not ready. And I probably never will be. I'm scared, Mum.

The downpour had been so strong that I couldn't distinguish the old woman's tears from the raindrops. It was as if they were already one. As if it no longer mattered whether they fell from the sky or her eyes. Her husband had hugged her tightly, with lips barely touching her hair.

"Everything will be fine," he kept repeating. "We'll see her again soon."

I don't know whether he wanted to comfort his wife or if he was trying to comfort himself. But whatever the reason, they both knew the time had come to let their daughter fly away from home. She was no longer the little girl who never wanted to play with dolls. She would say that the trolleys and trains were much more fun. You didn't have to imagine what they were and what they would become when they grew up. They were just cars and trains waiting for a curious child to pick them up and breathe life into them.

She was definitely an interesting child, very different from her peers.

I didn't know the old couple very well. We always greeted each other when we saw one another, sometimes stopped and talked, but we were never officially introduced. Maybe there was no need. What would knowing some names we had no choice in change?

They lived in the building next door to the orphanage. And same as me, they loved spending time in the nearby park, where we ran into each other almost every day. Their daughter grew up in front of my eyes. They aged in front of my eyes, and I grew up in front of theirs.

That day, there was only the two of them sitting side by side on one of the benches that held so many memories.

The park didn't seem the same that day. Something was missing. Even I could feel it.

The little blonde girl had gone elsewhere. She had grown up and chosen her own path. Not even a day had passed since she left to study in Switzerland, and already it was clear they missed her very much.

On that very day, I think I learned an important lesson. Some of us are afraid of taking responsibility, others are afraid of what would happen to them when that responsibility disappears, and others are afraid that they'll never have the chance to experience such responsibility.

But no matter how different we are, what we all have in common is that we all feel fear. I'm scared today too, Mum. And I'll probably be afraid tomorrow, and the days after, and maybe even for the rest of my life.

The nurse has just arrived. The blood test results are ready. Would you wish us luck, Mum? I hope it's not too late.

PS: Mum? I love you.

Love, Philip

One sent letter, two rings, three children, and dozens of sleepless nights later.

I've won!

Lately, life has been a little askew.

I asked life why you didn't love me, and it began explaining that you like vanilla ice cream and I like chocolate. That you love to read, and the last thing I read was my weekly horoscope, in which it was written that you didn't love me. I wouldn't be able to tell if a fruit was rotten, while you'll always able to spot the best grapes.

I think I've won here.

Long story short, life told me it wouldn't work out with you. Like when my literature teacher told me that no one would read a single line of what I wrote.

But here you are reading this letter. Yes, it's true that I wrote 'URGENT' on the envelope instead of my name, which might have been just a bit misleading. But the important thing, in this case, is that you are reading this. That's why I will continue to love you! In spite of life.

And who knows? It may turn out that it was wrong too. But even if that isn't so, the important thing is that I have loved.
Love,
Philip

Love, Philip: continuation
*Because I'm stupid and stubborn,
and a letter isn't enough to prove it.*

I often talk to you… even though you aren't here. I tell you about my day. Like the other day when I almost got into a fight with an old man, who allegedly, without wanting, hit me twice on the leg with his cane. And on top of that, the kid in front of me in the queue got the last 'Snickers' bar! And I really, please believe me, wanted that 'Snickers'.

What was that kid's problem? If only he had gotten a 'Twix' bar or a chocolate egg or something. We are flooded with an abundance of all kinds of sweets and candies, but no… no, he wanted exactly that 'Snickers'. And just when I thought it couldn't get any worse, the cashier said she was done for the day, and we had to move to another checkout. Can you imagine? They robbed me, beat me up, and kicked me out.

OK, maybe I'm exaggerating a bit, but it sure wasn't my day. But on the other hand, it was good that there were so many things to tell you, and you laughed without even taking a breath. Or at least, that's how I imagine you reacted.

Tell me honestly, please. Is it crazy? Is it crazy that I dream of coming home at night and telling you all these absurd stories? Is it crazy to believe that one day I'll unlock the front door, and you'll be there, furious that I haven't taken out the trash again and now the entire flat smells like... you get the idea. Please, be angry with me. Please, be here. That's all I want.

Some people believe that everything in our lives happens for a reason, and nothing is by chance because our path is pre-charted, and one way or another, everything leads us to the destiny that the world has assigned to us. It might be so. Tell it to my heart, though. Life said we weren't meant to be together, but my heart... well, it totally disagrees. A man wants exactly what he cannot have. That's what everyone says, but the problem is that I don't want to possess you. I want to see your smile when you're telling a story that isn't really all that funny... but to you, it is. And that's the most important thing to me. I want to hear once again how you failed to hit the high note on the refrain of your favourite song. As long as you're happy, I'm happy.

OK, it's crazy, I agree. But now I don't seem to miss you so much. You didn't hear a word of it, you didn't even realise I was talking to you... but somehow, I feel relieved. So fate can go... you can guess where. Because it's my heart alone that knows the right path, and I will follow it.

The trap

Hello, dear Mum.

Today, I am writing to tell you about a kind of sense which I call 'the trap'. Growing up in a home for orphans, I felt that feeling every day; at night when I was falling asleep, in the mornings when I just woke up. I had grown accustomed to that feeling. It had become part of me.

I was surrounded by so many other children, and yet I felt so lonely. How would you describe loneliness, Mum? Have you ever felt that way? For me, loneliness is like a trap that we fall into, and the more we try to get out, the more the walls closed in. And when there is nowhere to wiggle, you sit down quietly on the ground with your knees folded up to your chest and begin waiting. Waiting for someone to come, to give you a hand, and to get you out of this trap. The only thing left is being yourself and the spark of hope that still smoulders in you.

Theodora was that hope for me. She gave me a hand and dragged me out from the trap of loneliness. I wondered how to thank her. And her? She just smiled at me. How could I forget that smile, Mum? I'll never forget it. Everything beamed for a moment, and the whole world was getting better and more beautiful.

Trivial, isn't it? Well, it is. But from that moment onward, my heart and soul finally relaxed. Anxiety and loneliness had gone so far away from me. I was not alone anymore! It was as if I had wings on my shoulders, and I wanted to live so much! I realised how happy people felt. Wonderful.

But today, dear Mum, I'm not a happy person. The trap, which I thought I had already escaped from forever, stands in front of me again. Once again, I had stepped wrong and fell into it.

You would ask "How?" How did I happen to get caught in the same trap for a second time? I don't know, Mum. In one moment, I'm moving forward, and in the next, I'm falling straight down. But today, the difference is that Theodora can't help me get me out. In fact, she is with me here, in the trap: shackled in her own chains. She is here but powerless and helpless like me. When I ask her how she's feeling today, she just shakes her head, staring at the ground. Let's go out for a walk, I say, to get some fresh air. And she replies that she is tired. Of course, she is tired; she neither eats food nor drinks water. I'm trying to understand, Mum. I really am… but sometimes I can't. Today I gave her two slices of apple.

"Take them," I said. "You'll feel better".

And she remained silent, only shaking her head.

Then something in me pushed with such force that I couldn't stop it. "What do you want from me? Why are you silent? Why do you hurt me in such a way? Don't you see that it hurts me?"

But she remained silent and didn't shift her gaze.

I grabbed her shoulders. "Look at me! Look at me! Can you hear me? You are killing yourself, but you are killing me, too!"

As soon as I spoke those words, I fell to my knees, and dozens of pieces of broken china plates were around me. Tears streamed down my face, and I could not stop them. Theodora rose slightly and, without looking at me, left the room.

As soon as the door closed behind her, remorse filled my soul. How could I be so selfish? Well, but she was ill. Was this the way to take care of her? Was this the way to help her? At that moment, my heart broke, Mum. Everything in me and around me had become a thousand pieces.

Today, Mum, I am writing to you with just these questions: How can I sleep peacefully tonight, and how am I supposed to keep fighting when morning comes?

Dear Mum, help me. I'm all alone, fighting for two lives. I'm afraid.

The dreams

Hi, dear Mum!

How are you today? Are you OK? Is something bothering you? Are you happy?

Don't answer, Mum. I didn't plan to write to you today.

I didn't even want to think about you because my head was full of so many other thoughts and countless questions which I couldn't answer myself.

But I had no choice.

Today, like every other day, you are in my dreams, although we have never met face to face, eye to eye.

You are so far from me, yet at the same time, you are always here in my thoughts. Today, I am writing to you from the bus, Line 22, which crosses almost the entire city before reaching its final point: the Central Hospital.

We passed my stop long ago.

The bus has already made a U-turn and is heading back to its starting point, ready to run along the painfully familiar route once again today.

Mum, I didn't get off the bus. I wanted to stay a little longer here on the warm seat, talking to you.

When I got on the bus, a mother and daughter were sitting on the seat next to me. The girl was about eight to nine years old. She was quiet and quite tame, not typical for a young child. And that wasn't just my impression. After a short moment of complete silence, the mother turned to her daughter and asked if she was OK, if she felt bad, and why was she so silent? With a sincere childish smile, the girl said:

"I'm just dreaming."

How fabulous that sounds, Mum.

I'm just dreaming.

At that moment, I remembered the words of one of the educators at the orphanage. Whenever dreams and future

ATAHAC—77

plans had been discussed, no matter how rarely the subject had been brought up, she always said the same thing: *"Dreams are free for everyone."*

And it's good, Mum! It's good that at least dreams are free in this world! What do you need? Just close your eyes, and you'll have everything you've ever wished for. Everything, Mum.

Everything.

I know what some nauseatingly positive-minded people would say from their perspective on life. They would convince me that you could achieve whatever you wanted as long as you truly wanted it and fought to the end. No… I'm not making fun of them, Mum.

That's right. They're probably right.

Perhaps people who think this way can make their dreams come true. But I'll ask you, Mum. You and all people.

Tell me how, even while having endless faith and struggling hard, can I have a mother?

How can you be by my side, Mum?

How can I bring back the sleepless nights? The nights when I woke up shaking from yet another nightmare. The nights when I just wanted to get up, go to your bed, and snuggle. There… There, with *my mother*, where it's safest.

That's why I learned something. Something everyone knows how to do and probably loves as much as I do.

I learned to dream.

I would sit somewhere quiet, away from the other children, close my eyes or just stare out somewhere at empty space. Then, the miracle happened. You were standing next to me. And I was bouncing tirelessly around you, bombarding you with thousands of questions that I couldn't even wait to hear the answer to.

In that moment, however brief it was, I had a family. As if everything was real.

That is why I love dreams so much. Yes, maybe because it's easier. Sometimes, I even wish I wasn't in reality and could live there, in my dreams, where everything is exactly as I would like it to be. Where I can pick up the phone and call you on a hard day. Where I know I'll always have your support.

Where Theodora isn't lying chained to a hospital bed with yet another catheter tightly penetrating her thin skin. Where the hospital room hasn't turned into my home. Where…

Goodbye, dear Mum.

My stop came around for the third time today.

See you soon, dear Mum. I'll see you, and we'll talk soon… hopefully. Someplace I'd have everything… where I'd have you!

Autumn
(Goodbye Teddy)

Do you love autumn, Mum?

The reddish-brown and yellow colours on the trees, the leaf-strewn sidewalks, the chestnuts that fall to the ground and get picked up by children who then compete on who can throw their chestnut the farthest.

Autumn, when everything seems to subside into a peaceful sleep, and the wind gently caresses our ears. Autumn, when there is always at least one carefully collected pile of yellowed leaves on every street, and the wind, as if defiantly, like a small child, blows again and scatters them onto the paved street.

Autumn, when they say everything dies. But why, Mum? Why does everything die? Is it to give birth to a new life? If the leaves do not fall now, then in the spring, how will we enjoy the new life? How will we enjoy the colourful flowers and fragrant lilacs carried like a gentle perfume on the streets full of people under the long-awaited sun? But autumn, Mum, autumn is my favourite season.

Exactly one year ago, I had walked down this paved street.

I saw a man with a hand-made broom gathering the leaves into a pile. I don't know why, Mum, but I stopped and watched him. With such calmness and a slight smile on his face, he collected the leaves as if it was the best activity. After he had collected a nice pile about half a meter high, he took a match out of a cardboard box, lit it, and threw it onto the leaves. It took him a while. He had to nudge the pile a little and light another match, but finally, the leaves caught fire. And slowly, they burned, spreading that very specific smell that wafts all over the city in autumn. That's my favourite smell, Mum. I can't quite explain it, but it seems to bring me a sense of peace and comfort that I can't find anywhere else. Theodora does not like this smell. Sometimes, she says it even gives her a headache. But she loved me and always stayed beside me on the bench while I closed my eyes, felt the wind on my face, and smiled, enjoying the scent of smoke wafting through the air. Autumn, a friendly hand to hold… I had it all.

At a time when people say the world is dying, I seem to have been born filled with a genuine thirst for life. As the leaves caught fire, the pleasant aroma of smoke wafting even stronger in the air, the man put the broom aside and sat down near the burning pile. I looked at him for a while, thinking he would move aside, but he didn't move. He stood there staring at the sparks flying from the fire. I couldn't hold back; I got up and approached him.

"Sorry to bother you. I just wanted to make sure you were OK. Aren't you too close to the fire?"

He laughed, removed the cigarette butt from his mouth and threw it to the ground.

"I am addicted to fragrance. I have been collecting leaves and burning them for years. And every year, I look forward to autumn again. I'm used to it."

I smiled too because I understood. There was nothing better than autumn. I raised my hand in farewell and turned to leave.

"My condolences," he told me.

I felt horror, but at the same time, a look of astonishment crossed my face.

He lifted his hand slightly and pointed to the upper left side of my blouse. The little black ribbon fluttered slightly in the autumn wind. I smiled politely and nodded my head.

One day, Mum. It was the first day she was gone forever. I promised myself not to cry, Mum. I promised myself to be strong. Because of her, Mum, because of my truest friend. Except at night.

Then it's forgiven. Then even the strongest allow themselves to be weak. At night, when it is so dark that no one can see our tears, and in the morning, when the sun rises again, there is no trace of them. At night… At night, everyone cries, Mum. You probably do as well.

The man began to speak in a slightly hoarse voice, probably thick from inhaled smoke.

"My grandfather… My grandfather loved autumn even more than I did. My family had lost almost everything. We had no money for food, and as a sixth grader, I would help an artisan in exchange for bread or cheese to take home. When we were on the brink of poverty, my grandfather would collect the leaves in the yard in a big pile and set them on fire. He would sit next to the flame, and I would sit on his lap while he told me stories. All kinds of tales, about animals, about people, about monsters and creatures never seen before. All sorts of stories I don't even remember. But I do remember one thing: every story ended the same way.

'You see, my boy,' he'd say to me, 'sometimes everything has to go bad, fall apart and lose everything in order for things to be made right.'"

Then he stared again at the burning leaves and said no more. I timidly extended my hand and waved goodbye. As I walked away, the scent of burning leaves left a fainter and fainter but never-fading memory in my mind. I love autumn, Mum. Waiting for spring. Because if we don't lose everything today, tomorrow we won't know what it's like to have had everything.

PS: Goodbye, dear Teddy.

Note: As I say a few lines down, Mum, sooner or later, everyone writes letters. And sooner or later, everyone will receive such a letter.

It was very hard for me to read those words and probably even harder to share them… even with you. I'll start first… before I share the letter I received.

There is something about writing letters that is so comforting. Nothing changes from the moment you pick up the paper yellowed by sunlight to the moment you write the final letter of the last word. You rush so much as if you were trying to catch your own thoughts, which run tirelessly, and your hand cannot keep up. Large, legible letters turn into scribbles that are barely comprehensible to the author themself because there is almost no space left on the only sheet available, and there are still words and thoughts that have not been fully spoken and written. But you can't put down the slightly gnawed pencil because you know that if you stop to rummage through the drawers for some abandoned notebook, the words will disappear; they will simply evaporate as if they were never there. That moment of inspiration will once again melt into nothingness, and who knows how much longer those unspoken words and thoughts will remain locked away somewhere in this place called 'soul'?

An unreal world in a very real human body. Unreal longings, feelings, and dreams in a completely real world. I don't want to lose them, Mum. I do not want to. Because sometimes they're all I have left…

Nothing changes from the moment you pick up the sheet, slightly yellowed by the sunlight, to the moment you write the last letters of the last word…, but it feels as if everything has changed. The heaviness in your chest seems to have disappeared, or perhaps you yourself have become stronger.

Now you can take a deep breath again and make room for hope, for beautiful dreams. Nothing changes in the real world, but everything is different here in the other world, protected by the strong walls of our chests. This is probably why people write letters.

The hardest part was when I had to get the old leather suitcase out of the attic. It was covered in dust, and its wheels were completely worn out and barely turned. It was not one of the new, modern, lightweight suitcases that are easy to carry. It had a short handle that didn't extend, and carrying it down the old attic staircase was a real challenge. Why was this wooden batten placed over the last step? It didn't support anything; it was completely unnecessary. I hit it for the third time already, but it was unlikely to make my already terrible headache worse.

When I finally managed to drag the suitcase to the bedroom and set it down in front of the wooden wardrobe, I thought the hard part was over, but in fact, it was just beginning.

Dear Mum, have you packed for someone who is no longer there? You feel like you're sending them on an endless journey that you know they'll never come back from. Do you understand me, Mum? The pale pink vest she wore to that exhibition where the artist himself got so drunk that at the end of the night, he climbed onto the table with two forks in hand and conducted an orchestra consisting of a DJ and a karaoke singer. The dark green, cherry-stained pants she wore when we watched that insanely boring movie. Mum, have you ever eaten cherries during a movie? Neither had I, but it turned out to be even better than eating popcorn.

The snow-white sweater she wore only once. The park was strewn with yellow-reddish autumn leaves. She bent down and picked up a leaf, and said, "This is the most beautiful thing!" She took a small safety pin from her pocket and pinned it like a brooch on the left side of this blouse, right next to her heart.

And I thought it would be easy. I would fight the ever-nagging zipper. I would open the suitcase and quickly throw all the clothes inside… without thinking, without adding any emotion. But garment after garment, the memories surfaced one after the other, clearer than ever.

Of course, like any cupboard, this one had some unnecessary things that I just had to get rid of. I took the crumpled-up sheet of paper, and just before I tossed it into a plastic waste bag, I unfolded it and… and it was a letter.

Sooner or later, everyone writes letters. And sooner or later, everyone will receive such a letter.

From Theodora

My dear friend,

I don't know how to start. I am not one to pour out my thoughts and feelings. I'm not always prepared with a notebook and pen at hand like you. I don't know where to start and…

Probably, if I wasn't writing this letter specifically to you, then I would likely be asking you every five minutes: "What should I write now?"

Darling…

It hurts me. It's like my whole life has turned into numbers. The lower, the better.

But when the numbers go up, it's like I lose everything. I can't control it. And no one and nothing can help me.

I wake up thinking about what I'm going to have for breakfast. And before I've even had it, I'm already wondering what I'm going to eat for lunch so that I don't exceed my 'allowed' calories. If nothing else, at least my maths skills have improved over the past months of non-stop calculations. (I'm trying to joke; you've told me that every story, no matter how sad it is, needs a little humour, like the basil you sprinkle onto every meal. Seriously, stop it!)

For a long time, I didn't want to admit it, even to myself, but food became everything I had, everything that separated me from the world around me.

And from you.

But you never left me. You didn't turn around and walk away. And instead, you're here by my side, letting me drag you into this endless hell. I have asked myself many times why you do it when there is an easier way. Look at me—I'm selfish. Me, me, me… It's only *me* lately.

But believe me… I never wanted it to happen this way. I never wanted this, all this, to happen to you. However, it is stronger than me. It seized me and imprisoned me with its shackles, and I couldn't escape. The more I tried, the more the metal wires sank into my body and grew tighter and tighter.

It is stronger than me. It is stronger than us.

'It' begins with a capital A.

I'm so, so sorry.

Teddy

The cause "Theodora"

Hello Mum,

Eighty-four days have passed since Teddy died.

I don't try to count them, I don't even want to, but I just wake up every morning with a new number. Pain is a strange thing. I can't describe it. Some days, it's so strong that it seems to be suffocating me, and everything around me is slowly but surely collapsing. And other days, it seems to be gone; in fact, it's like I have absolutely no feelings at all. It's like someone snuck up in the night and ripped out my heart, then replaced it with some modern semblance of one that keeps me alive but doesn't allow me to feel any emotion. I don't know which of the two is scarier, but I know I'm scared, Mum. Sometimes I wonder if the pain is the same for everyone; does everyone suffer in the same way, or is the grief individual to the person?

Yesterday I passed by mine and Theodora's favourite shop. They sold almost everything there: clothes, toys, books, souvenirs, china cups and plates, jewellery, and even ink tapes for my typewriter. There was everything you could imagine in this shop.

The record for our longest time spent there (Theodora and I) was four hours and thirty-five minutes. But for me, it had seemed like only a moment. In fact, every moment with Theodora felt like just a second; time flew by, and she kept smiling and smiling. I was holding a small ceramic figure of a dog with disproportionately long ears and short legs, and I was convincing her how nice it would be to put it on the small table in our living room next to the other unnecessary trinkets that I had already bought from this same shop. And she just laughed, shook her head and agreed. Not that she actually agreed, but she knew it would make me happy, and it was the only way to avoid me grumbling all the way home. I hadn't been in the shop since Teddy left; it just wasn't the same. The shop itself was not the same; even the overpowering smell of cinnamon candles and old books was gone. I queued up at the register, holding one of Theodora's favourite books. I already had a copy and even read it several times, but this was an older edition with a hard, light brown cover and pages yellowed by time.

In front of me, a little girl was queuing. She looked no more than five years old, and her mother, judging by her puffy eyes, hadn't slept for at least two days. Waiting for them outside of the shop was a medium-sized shepherd-like dog, howling so loudly and pitifully that it could be heard inside. His howl was joined by the resounding cry of the little girl who clutched a knitted doll tightly in her arms, not about to give her up. And everyone around them stared at the young mother who, with the last of her patience and strength, was trying to calm her daughter down, unloading things from her basket, rummaging through her handbag, desperately searching for her wallet, and repeatedly apologising to the cashier and all the queuing people for the inconvenience and noise. There wasn't much to see but a tired woman holding the world on her shoulders.

Clutching the book tightly to my chest, I looked outside and then at the mother and the little girl in front of me. Our lives, our fates were so different, but as I had said, pain is a strange thing. Sometimes you can find it in the cry of a child who didn't get the knitted doll she wanted so much, in the whimper of a dog tied to the metal post in front of the shop, waiting for its owner, behind the tired eyes of the mother who just needed a moment of silence, or in the grieving heart of the girl with a book in her hand who had lost her best friend.

I could tell you many things about my friendship with Theodora, but I will only tell you one thing.

We entered the hallway, and my heart was beating so hard I felt like it was going to burst with worry. We looked at the list hanging on the door, and she slowly swiped her finger through all the names until suddenly… suddenly, my name was there. I was accepted at university to study writing, Mum. Can you believe it? Because, Mum, I couldn't believe it! I was

so happy that, for a moment, I might have been the happiest person in the world. Then Theodora turned to me with a look filled with infinite admiration and respect as if I were the first man to walk on the moon returning to Earth where people were waiting with bated breath to hear my every word. That was exactly how she looked at me, and that was exactly how I felt myself. But you should know, Mum, not every day was like this one. There are days when we aren't heroes. Days when I was everything but a hero.

The sun cut through the light green curtain, and I squeezed my eyes tighter and tighter, and my head twisted to the side. These were one of those days where I wanted to stop time and hide from the world, at least for a day or two, and sometimes even longer. Theodora sat down beside me with a cup of warm milk in her hand, removed the blanket from my face, caressed my forehead, and looked at me with the same look of admiration as the day when I had been accepted at university.

That's all I can tell you about my friendship with Theodora, Mum.

On the days when I returned victorious to the Earth and on the days when I didn't even want to open my eyes in the morning, she never stopped looking at me with admiration, not even for a moment. That was Theodora, Mum.

Do you know what is the most valuable thing for a writer? The most precious thing is the reader. No, no, I'm not talking about the famous authors with millions of books sold all over the world, social networks filled with hundreds or thousands of followers, and even 'urgently important' engagements and meetings. Not that I don't like them, Mum, quite the contrary. But as my favourite writer said in a very personal letter to the world: Being a writer is a dream. But I didn't start writing to become an author. I started writing because it was the only way to silence the voices in my mind… Being a writer and being an author are two very different things… I love to write because one is a writer when one writes. But being an author… it's a career now.

I don't think I could have said it any better, Mum. I'm one

of those people who dreams of being a writer. The other side of it is just not for me. But as I mentioned before, the most valuable thing is loyal readers. The ones who will look impatiently over your shoulder before you've even finished writing your last sentence, the ones who will spill coffee on your notes and then make you a biscuit cake with lots and lots of cream as an apology, the ones who will always give their honest opinion and support you on the days when you wrote your most beautiful words and on those days when you wrote the biggest nonsense; such complete nonsense that reading it the next day, you yourself would try to understand what happened to your brain to decide that the comparison between love and a herd of zebras was a good idea.

I tried to think of something to back up my reasoning at the time, but I still didn't have anything to say in my defence. But what's important here are those people who don't care if you're an author or a writer; they care about you and your words.

And that was Theodora to me, my best friend and my most faithful reader and admirer.

That's why I created this organisation for kids who love to write. And the truth is that sometimes everyone needs to write something. At least sometimes. To collect his or her thoughts, to understand himself or herself, and to share his or her pain, even if no one else will read it. I dedicated this cause to Theodora.

Well, dear mother…

Perhaps you might see this book on a shelf in the far corner of a bookshop because that's where the writers stand. Far from the showcase where the authors stand. But I will let you in on a secret that few people know. The writers' spot is actually the best one in the entire bookshop.

Few books get there, but the ones that do can always be found by those they were written for and those who need them. Something like a secret society of readers that no one knows about, not even the participants themselves.

It's so beautiful, Mum.

Love Your Book

Letters to you, to her, to no one

TIMELINE

AUGUST 2023

Soft-back book printed from paper that has been carbon offset through the World Land Trust Scheme.

PRINTED by Hobbs the Printers Ltd
at Southampton, United Kingdom

PUBLISHED by Cybirdy Publishing
London, United Kingdom

SPECIAL EDITION
Autographed by the Author

VASILENA SPASOVA

Cherish your book

WHO are you?	WHO did you obtain the book from?	WHEN did you obtain the book
FIRST GUARDIAN		
SECOND GUARDIAN		
THIRD GUARDIAN		
FOURTH GUARDIAN		
FIFTH GUARDIAN		

Vasilena Spasova is a native Bulgarian who was accepted at Brunel University in London, where she majored in Theatre, Film and Television. She furthered her education by undertaking a Master's in Creative Writing in 2017.

Letters to you, to her, to no one is her debut novel which she first published in Bulgarian in 2021 before releasing this translated version in English.

She currently lives in Bulgaria with her two dogs and three cats and is happily working on her next writing project.